Copyright © 2016 Annie Ni Bhroin

Illustrated by Gina Song

All rights reserved.

ISBN: 978-1-5272-0406-5

THIS BOOK BELONGS TO

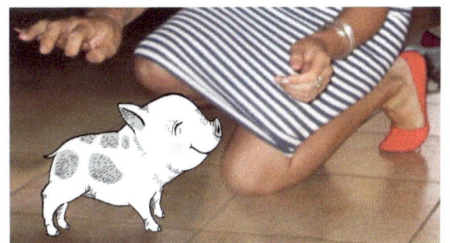

THOUGHTS ARE JUST
THOUGHTS.

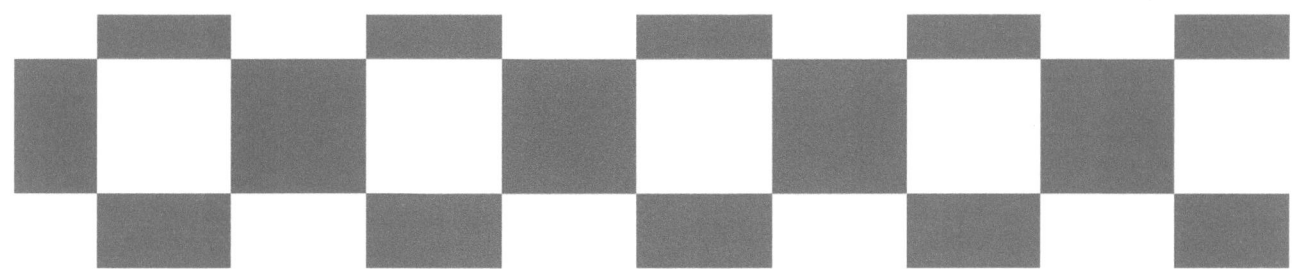

WHEN THEY COME, SAY
'HI!'

JUST LET 'EM GO, SAY
'BYE!'

Malachy was a micro-pig.

A teeny-tiny, little, cutesy baby pig!

Well that's what everyone else saw him as.

You see the problem was, Malachy didn't think very much of himself at all.

He didn't have many friends. He did most things alone.

He would skateboard alone.

He would eat alone.

He would play football alone.

He even went into town alone.

One day Anna Banana approached him and asked why he had no friends.

"It might be because I'm so small?" Malachy replied.

"It could be that I'm just not fun."

"Maybe it's because I'm not cool like the other micro-pigs."

In fact, he was simply tired of being Malachy.

"I'm tired of being me!"

Anna Banana decided she had the solution.

"You need to make friends with yourself first!"

"What on earth could she mean?" Malachy thought.

"All these thoughts you are having - well they're just thoughts! You need to let those thoughts go and calm your mind. I can help you!'

Anna Banana fetched her glitter mind jar. She had made it herself.

She gave it a good 'ol shake.

Wow, the glitter moved about inside the jar reflecting all the light.

But not for long....as the moments passed the glitter started to settle.

"It's just like your mind you see. All those thoughts just bouncing around inside.

After a little while, those thoughts settle too.

It really helps me stay calm when my thoughts are bouncing around. You try!"

Malachy gave it a shake. He watched the glitter as it swirled around and around, but sure enough, it started to slow down.

He noticed he didn't have so many of those thoughts.

Or maybe he did, he just let them pass. He liked watching the glitter fall slowly to the bottom.

"And just like with your skateboarding", she said, "It takes practice."

Malachy made his very own glitter mind jar.

When he started to get those thoughts about being alone and having no friends, he would shake his little jar and watch it settle, and over time, it seemed to work.

Malachy liked himself again.

You know what?

It was safe to say he had made friends with himself...

....and with Anna Banana,

...and Tommy Terrapin,

Oh, and everyone at the bus stop!

Do it yourself Glitter Mind jar!

You will need:
- jam jar
- glitter glue
- food colouring
- glitter – lots!

Step 1
Fill the jar half way with hot water from the tap (definitely an adults job!)

Step 2
Add in a few generous squirts of glue and mix well with a spoon

Step 3
Add in a few drops of food colouring

Step 4
Add in the glitter – go nuts!

Step 5
Fill jar to the top with remaining water.

Step 6
Put the lid on and give it a good shake. (You might want to glue it closed)

Step 7
Enjoy!

ABOUT THE AUTHOR

Annie is an educator and enthusiastic meditator. She discovered the value of mindfulness for small children during her time as a primary school teacher in London (and as a devoted auntie!) She learned many techniques to create a calm and positive environment for kids to explore their little worlds.